Saint Anthony of Padua

◆ The Story of His Life and Popular Devotions

CINCINNATI, OHIO

Nihil Obstat: Rev. Nicholas Lohkamp, O.F.M.
Rev. Edward J. Gratsch

Imprimi Potest: Rev. John Bok, O.F.M.
Provincial

Imprimatur: +R. Daniel Conlon
Archdiocese of Cincinnati
February 2, 1993

The *nihil obstat* and *imprimatur* are a declaration that a book is considered to be free from doctrinal or moral error. It is not implied that those who have granted the *nihil obstat* and *imprimatur* agree with the contents, opinions or statements expressed.

Cover and book design by Nancy Hopkins

ISBN 0-86716-202-3

Published by St. Anthony Messenger Press
Printed in the U.S.A.

Contents

Introduction

A favorite in much of the Catholic world, St. Anthony of Padua has more cities and places named after him than any other saint—sixty-eight. This includes forty-four in Latin America, fifteen in the United States, four in Canada and the Philippines, and one in Spain. Four capes, three bays, two reefs and two peaks take his name.

Even more numerous have been, until recently, the statues of St. Anthony in churches depicting him holding the Christ Child, the book of Scriptures, a flaming torch or a lily.

Obviously the saint must have been a favorite of missionaries who came to the Western hemisphere. But over the years it seems to have been laypeople who have adopted St. Anthony of Padua as a kind of all-purpose saint—finder of lost articles, helper in troubles, healer of bodies and spirits. Hundreds of thousands have prayed the quaint old responsory: "If miracles thou fain would see, Lo, error, death, calamity...."

We might be tempted to ask, as a friar once asked St. Francis of Assisi, "Why after you? Why after you?" The answer seems to be both the immense popularity of St. Anthony in his lifetime and the flood of wonders that followed his death.

In *St. Anthony: Doctor of the Church* (Franciscan Press/Quincy College) Franciscan scholar Sophronius Clasen wrote: "Immediately after his death, Anthony became the object of an extraordinary devotion; and miracle followed miracle, as the prayers of the sick and afflicted were answered by sudden cures and other wonders. This set on foot a great wave of enthusiasm, and drew large crowds to his tomb, who began to honor him as a Saint even before the Pope had canonized him. Often orderly processions were formed; and these were led sometimes by the bishop of Padua and his clergy. The leading knights of the city and the students of the university all took part; and all carried candles of great size."

Part One:
Who Is St. Anthony?

Finding the Real St. Anthony

♦ *By Leonard Foley, O.F.M.*

*O*lder, unremodeled churches most always count St. Anthony among their pantheon of statues. The saint of Padua is usually sculpted or portrayed holding the child Jesus—or a lily—or a book—or all three—in his arms. A bank of vigil lights will burn in front of the statue.

Tuesday evening is the traditional time of St. Anthony novena devotions, with prayers to St. Anthony, Benediction and the reading of petitions written on little scraps of paper: "for a safe delivery," "to obtain a job," "for reconciliation with my daughter," and, invariably, "to find my lost _____." On the saint's feast day, June 13, St. Anthony Bread is blessed. And since the saint is the special patron of Italy, an honor he shares with St. Francis, many Italian families have a son named Anthony.

The list of human concerns for which Anthony is the patron is amazingly varied. Father Lothar Hardick, O.F.M., who recently wrote a book on the saint, tells us that St. Anthony has been known as the patron of lovers and of marriage, as a helper in time of birth or as a help against infertility. He was called upon against fevers, against diabolic powers and against plagues among cattle. He was honored as the patron of mariners as well as those who live in mountainous areas. The familiar responsory says:

> If then you ask for miracles
> Death, error, all calamities,
> The leprosy and demons fly,
> And health succeeds infirmities.
>
> The sea obeys and fetters break,
> And lifeless limbs thou dost restore,
> Whilst treasures lost are found again
> When young or old thine aid implore.
>
> All dangers vanish at thy prayer,
> And every need doth quickly flee.
> Let those who know thy power proclaim—
> Let Paduans say, "These are of thee."

The array of wonders attributed to Anthony in story and legend is equally astounding in its variety. He was in two places at the same time; at his prayer, a donkey knelt before the Blessed Sacrament, after a dare by an unbeliever; fishes lifted their heads above the water to listen as he preached to them, after bored believers turned away; a foot severed by an ax was rejoined to its leg.

Are these legends true? Let us first see if we can trace the line of facts regarding this immensely popular saint.

Anthony = Fernando Bulhom

Sophronius Clasen, O.F.M., has written an excellent biography of St. Anthony: *St. Anthony: Doctor of the Church*. The following summary is based on that source.

Anthony was born in 1195 (thirteen years after St. Francis) in Lisbon (now Portugal, then a part of Spain), at the mouth of the Tagus River, from which explorers would later sail across the Atlantic. His parents, Martin and Mary Bulhom, apparently belonged to one of the prominent families of the city, and were among those who had been loyal in service to the king. The infant was baptized in the nearby cathedral at the foot of Castle Sao Jorge, which still dominates the city. He was given the name *Fernando*.

He attended the cathedral school and at the surprisingly young age of fifteen entered the religious order of St. Augustine. "Whoever enters a monastery," he later wrote, "goes, so to speak, to his grave." For Fernando, however, the monastery was far from peaceful because his old friends came to visit so frequently. Their vehement political discussions hardly provided an atmosphere for prayer and study.

After two years of this, the young man asked to move and was sent to Coimbra, one hundred miles north. This was the beginning of nine years of intense study, learning the Augustinian theology which he would later combine with the Franciscan vision. Fernando was probably ordained a priest during this time.

Firmly Against Heresy, Warmly Toward Truth

The life of this young priest took a crucial turn when the bodies of the first five Franciscan martyrs were returned from Morocco. They had preached in the mosque in Seville, almost being martyred at the outset, but the sultan allowed them to pass on to Morocco, where, after continuing to preach Christ despite repeated warnings, they were tortured and beheaded. Now, in the presence of the queen and a huge crowd, their remains were carried in solemn procession to Fernando's monastery.

He was overjoyed and inspired to a momentous decision. He went to the little friary the queen had given the Franciscans in Coimbra and said, "Brother, I would gladly put on the habit of your Order if you would promise to send me as soon as possible to the land of the Saracens, that I may gain the crown of the holy martyrs." After some challenges from the prior of the Augustinians, he was allowed to leave that priory and receive the Franciscan habit, taking the name *Anthony*, after the patron of their local church and friary, St. Anthony of the Olives. He was allowed to take vows immediately, since the Order did not yet require a novitiate.

True to their promise, the friars allowed Anthony to go to Morocco, to be a witness for Christ, and a martyr as well. But, as often happens, the gift he wanted to give was not the gift that was to be asked of him. He became seriously ill, and after several months realized he had to go home.

He never arrived. His ship ran into storms and high winds and was blown east across the Mediterranean. Months later, he arrived on the east coast of Sicily, a thousand miles east. The friars at nearby Messina, though they didn't know him, welcomed him and began nursing him back to health. Still ailing, he wanted to attend the great Pentecost Chapter of Mats (so called because the three thousand friars could not be housed and slept on mats). Francis was there, also sick. History does not reveal any meeting between Francis and Anthony. Since the young man was from "out of town," he received no assignment at the meeting, so he asked to go with a provincial superior from northern Italy. "Instruct me in the Franciscan life," he asked, not mentioning his prior theological training. Now, like Francis, he had his first choice—a life of seclusion and contemplation in a little hermitage near Montepaolo.

Perhaps we would never have heard of him if he hadn't gone to an ordination of Dominicans and Franciscans in 1222. As they gathered for a meal afterward, the provincial suggested that one of the friars give a short sermon. Quite typically, everybody ducked. So Anthony was asked to give "just something simple," since he presumably had no education.

Anthony too demurred, but finally began to speak in a simple, artless way. The fire within him became evident. His knowledge was unmistakable, but his holiness was what really impressed everyone there.

Now he was exposed. His quiet life of prayer and penance at the hermitage was exchanged for that of a public preacher. Francis heard of Anthony's previously hidden gifts, and Anthony was assigned to preach in northern Italy. It was not like preaching around Assisi, where the faith was strong: Here he ran into heretics, well organized and ardent.

The problem with many preachers in Anthony's day was that their life-style contrasted sharply with that of the poor people to whom they preached. In our experience, it could be compared to an evangelist arriving in a slum driving a Mercedes, delivering a homily from his car and speeding off to a vacation resort.

The heresy of that time thus had its grain of truth. The so-called "Pure" (Cathari) began by wanting to go back to gospel poverty. Scandalized by the wealth of the Church, they practiced strict poverty and engaged in manual labor. But they also denied the validity of the hierarchy and the sacraments. They saw themselves as the only "real" Christians.

Anthony saw that words were obviously not enough. He had to *show* them gospel poverty. People wanted more than self-disciplined, even penitent, priests. They wanted the unselfish genuineness of gospel living. And in Anthony they found it. They were moved by who he was, more than what he said. In Rimini, one hotbed of heresy, he was able to call the people together—that alone was a sign of his fame.

Despite his efforts, not everyone listened. Legend has it that one day, faced with deaf ears, Anthony went to the river and preached to the fishes. That, reads the traditional tale, got *everyone's* attention.

Anthony traveled tirelessly in both northern Italy and southern France—perhaps four hundred trips—choosing to enter the cities where the heretics were strongest. Yet the sermons he has left behind rarely show him taking direct issue with the heretics. As the historian Clasen interprets it, Anthony preferred to present the grandeur of Christianity in positive ways. It was no good to prove people *wrong*: Anthony wanted to win them to the *right*, the healthiness of real sorrow and conversion, the wonder of reconciliation with a loving Father. The word *fire* recurs in descriptions of him. And though he was called the "Hammer of Heretics," the word *warmth* describes him more fully.

Public Preacher, Franciscan Teacher

Anthony's superior, St. Francis, was cautious about education such as his protégé possessed. He had seen too many theologians taking pride in their sophisticated knowledge. Still, if the friars had to hit the roads and preach to all sorts of people, they needed a firm grounding in Scripture and theology. So, when he heard the glowing report of Anthony's debut at the ordinations, Francis wrote in 1224, "It pleases me that you should teach the friars sacred theology, provided that in such studies they do not destroy the spirit of holy prayer and devotedness, as contained in the Rule."

Anthony first taught in a friary in Bologna, which became a famous school. The theology book of the time was the Bible. In one extant sermon by the saint, there are at least 183 passages from

Scripture. While none of his theological conferences and discussions were written down, we do have two volumes of his sermons: *Sunday Sermons* and *Feastday Sermons*. His method included much of allegory and symbolical explanation of Scripture. This approach is not often used today, when the historical method is in vogue.

Nature was a fertile field from which Anthony gathered symbols and allegories—as did Jesus— like the lilies of the field, the nest of birds, the web of the spider, the last cry of the dying swan. But above all, Anthony made references to *fire*, which is why he is sometimes portrayed with a book (the Bible) in one hand and holding a flame toward the onlooker with the other.

On the occasion of St. Anthony being declared a doctor of the Church, the minister general of the Friars Minor, Valentine Schaaf, wrote: "Our Holy Doctor was the connecting link which joined the chain of the ancient Augustinian tradition [which Anthony had learned in Coimbra] to the then barely emerging Franciscan school.... After Anthony it was especially the Seraphic Doctor St. Bonaventure and the Venerable John Duns Scotus, the Subtle Doctor, who continued to adhere more rigidly and faithfully to the Augustinian spirit, which is briefly expressed in the following words: 'The fulfillment and the end of the Law and of all divine Scriptures is *love*.' Both unanimously assert that theology is a practical science insofar as it is the end of theology to move and lead man to love God."

Anthony continued to preach, as he taught the friars and assumed more responsibility within the Order. In 1226 he was appointed provincial superior of northern Italy, but still found time for contemplative prayer in a small hermitage. Around Easter in 1228 (he was only thirty-three years old), while in Rome, he met Pope Gregory IX, who had been a faithful friend and adviser of St. Francis. Naturally, the famous preacher was invited to speak. He did it humbly, as always. The response was so great that people later said that it seemed the miracle of Pentecost was repeated.

Padua Enters the Picture

Padua, Italy, is a short distance west of Venice. At the time of Anthony, it was one of the most important cities in the country, with an important university for the study of civil and canon law. Religion there was at a low point. There was constant fighting between the tyrant Ezzelino, a ruthless, brutal man who led the Ghibellines, and the Guelph party in Verona. Anthony divided his time between solitude to write the two volumes of his sermons and preaching to the people of Padua.

Sometimes he left Padua for greater solitude. He went to a place loved by Francis—LaVerna, where Francis received the wounds of Jesus. He also found a grotto near the friary where he could pray in silence and solitude.

In poor health, and still provincial superior of northern Italy, he went to the General Chapter in Rome and asked to be relieved. But he was later recalled as part of a special commission to discuss certain matters of the Franciscan Rule with the pope.

Back in Padua, he preached his last and most famous Lenten sermons. The crowds were so great—sometimes thirty thousand—that the churches could not hold them, so he went into the piazzas or the open fields. People waited all night to hear him. He needed a bodyguard to protect him from the people armed with scissors who wanted to snip off a piece of his habit as a relic. After his morning Mass and sermon, he would hear confessions. This sometimes lasted all day—as did his fasting.

Anthony was instrumental in a matter of social justice. Under the law, a Paduan debtor was put in prison if he could not pay. A new law read: "At the request of the venerable Friar (and holy confessor) Anthony of the Order of Friars Minor, it is established and ordained that henceforth no one is to be held in prison for pecuniary debt." Debtors did have to relinquish their possessions, but they were free. In another instance of civic involvement, he failed to move the tyrant Ezzelino to release the leader of those opposing him. Anthony was so disappointed over this that he withdrew from public life.

The great energy he had expended during Lent left him exhausted. He went to a little town near Padua, but seeing death coming close, he wanted to return to the city that he loved. "If it seems good to you," he said to one of the friars, "I should like to return to Padua to the friary of Santa Maria, so as not to be a burden to the friars here." The journey in a wagon weakened him so much, however, that he had to stop at Arcella. He had to bless Padua from a distance, as Francis had blessed Assisi.

At Arcella, he received the last sacraments, sang and prayed with the friars there. When one of them asked Anthony what he was staring at so intently, he answered, "I see my Lord!" He died in peace a short time after that. He was only thirty-six and had been a Franciscan but ten years.

The following year, his friend, Pope Gregory IX, moved by the many miracles that occurred at Anthony's tomb, declared him a saint. Many years later, during exhumation of Anthony's body for transferal, Anthony's tongue was found to be still lifelike and of a natural color, though the rest of his body had disintegrated. St. Bonaventure, head of all Franciscans in the world, was present at the transfer, and he cried out, "O blessed tongue, you have always praised the Lord and led others to praise him! Now we can clearly see how great indeed have been your merits before God!"

Anthony was a simple and humble friar who preached the Good News lovingly and with fearless courage. The youth whom his fellow friars thought was uneducated became one of the great preachers and theologians of his day. He was a man of great penance and apostolic zeal. But he was primarily a saint of the people.

Over-the-Back-Fence Theology

Devotion to Anthony began while he was still living and spread quickly after his death. Legends and stories of his life multiplied, as they often do with popular saints. The question arises: Which are true?

In our day, historians examine the past using a strictly scientific method. World-famous and most conscientious theologian Father Ignatius Brady, O.F.M., has written, "I may seem a bit 'modern' but there is no need to dwell on legends when there are so many proven miracles that have been worked by his [Anthony's] intercession.... The Christ-Child is closer to Anthony and all of us if we are living in God's grace than if he were a baby in our arms. So the story is still 'true' even if it is a legend."

Legends and stories are the poetry of childlike faith. They arise among people who feel no inhibition about using their imagination. Even as scientific hagiographers watch them over their glasses, they are not afraid to let the line between fact and story blur—it's practically impossible to find that line anyway. The poetry of the simple (a stumbling block to the wise) warms the solemn declarations of the creeds.

The makers of legend let their minds soar through the skies of wonder. They know the dogmas that are engraved in granite: Jesus is true God and true man; God is One and Trinity; we are saved by the death and resurrection of Jesus, re-presented at every Eucharist. But they are not loath to embellish the majestic picture of Jesus rising from the dead with little cherubs. If God wants you to find your false teeth through the prayer of St. Anthony, I say wonderful. *Deo gratias!*

By way of understanding the story-weaving of Catholic tradition, do you remember the Sisters teaching the story of the boy Jesus making sparrows out of mud? How he clapped his hands and they flew away? We've all heard that "St. Christopher" bore the infant Jesus over a raging stream: The name meant "Christ-bearer." We "know" there was a little door at the back of heaven where Mary let sinners in, after St. Peter wouldn't let them through the pearly gates. We recall that St. Scholastica prayed for rain, and the resulting flood from heaven made it impossible for her brother St. Benedict to leave her convent—which was her wish all the while. And so forth.

God forbid this would become the basis of faith

and we would ever abandon systematic and logical theology. It, after all, also uses the wide-ranging power of imagination. But it seems evident that human nature needs some over-the-back-fence theology that is not quite so stern and unrelieved— coffee-klatch poetry that suggests but does not prove. Legends are comforting where dogma is reassuring. And sometimes legends are just plain fun—something that should never be in short supply among the children of God.

Jesus *could have* made mud sparrows fly. Whether he actually met Peter sneaking out of Rome doesn't matter: His prescience was a challenge to Peter's conscience. Mary isn't in charge of a black-market back door to heaven, but she *is* a motherly symbol of the mercy of God. And *every* person who lifts another person's spirits and "carries" them through troubled times is named "Christopher" on those imaginary record books in heaven.

It's something like "My Dad can do anything!" which means, in concepts we may or may not have developed later, that I have a solid foundation under my life. There is Someone there who literally *can* do anything, One in whom I can trust absolutely. There *is* a Santa Claus, who works the year round.

Why St. Anthony?

It's easy to see why some saints attract people with
certain needs: Mary for both mothers and celibates,
Joseph for workers, (someday) Mother Teresa for
those who care for the most abandoned of the poor.
But what can explain the almost universal cult of St.
Anthony? He had no biographer like Thomas of
Celano, who wrote Francis' life a few years after he
died. In fact, apart from his dramatic early days,
when he was determined to be martyred by
Muslims, and the final glorious days in Padua, the
middle years seem like outlines: accounts of his
preaching, especially against the Albigensian
heresy (the "Pure" again) in Italy and France, and
complimentary generalities about his care for the
friars as provincial minister and member of the
General Counsel of the Order.

  We do have his sermons. But, apart from the
legends, his life was what every Christian's life is
meant to be, but writ large—a steady courage to
face the ups and downs of life, the call to love and
forgive, to be concerned for the needs of others, to
deal with crises great and small, and to have our
feet solidly on the ground of total, trusting love and
dependence on God.

Why his popularity, then? At least some of the stories must be literally true. He must have had an overpowering effect on the people of his day. He must have been an authentic saint.

The legends abound. Bring the fishes' heads above water. Have them dance, if you want to. Let the donkeys kneel down before Jesus, even sing the Our Father. *My Dad can do anything.*

But aren't there dangers here? Certainly. I have seen people enter a church, completely ignore the reserved sacrament and go directly to kneel before Anthony's statue. I have seen, in an Asian country, wall-to-wall people jamming the streets around a church on a weekday night when a certain novena was to be held. The following Sunday, the street was almost empty. I suppose there are people who, to put it bluntly, seem to have more faith in Anthony than in Jesus.

These practices certainly don't suit the saint they are intended to honor! The greatest danger is attributing to a saint what *only God can do*. No one can save your soul but God in Jesus and the Spirit. God's grace—that is, the total unconditional love surrounding every human being—comes only from God. We ask the saints in heaven to pray for us, just as we ask some earthly saints (and even some who may not qualify) to pray for us. But none of them "grants grace."

All right, some will say, in a familiar line of argument, why not go straight to God? Jesus is the universal and only savior. By all means, let us go to God first, make Jesus the center. But we are human, and God is invisible, and so is Jesus—for now. So God sends us brothers and sisters who are—or at least are called to be—warm, supportive, comforting. They make God's love visible—the ones still with us, and those who have gone ahead. They are sacraments—small "s"—of God's love.

Perhaps we may say that in the great river that is our faith and religion and the solid truths of revelation, there are some shallows next to the shore. These are the meandering legends and stories that feed the main stream. When it gets too deep for us, we can play along the side for a while. That's human and understandable, as long as we know the river's source.

There are overwhelming facts in Jesus' life, especially his miracles, his fearless denunciation of hypocrisy, his death and resurrection. But he also made 120 gallons of wine for a wedding celebration. And anyone who thinks he never played a trick or two on Joseph and Mary should take a course under Dr. Bill Cosby. I think St. Anthony would say about all the legends and stories: "Let's have balance, but imagination too, just as we have Shakespeare and 'Casey at the Bat'; Beethoven, but also a little schmaltz."

But St. Anthony of Padua would also say, "Fight error with courage and kindness. Look around you and see the injustice that chains so many people. Take time for quiet prayer. Know your faith and let that knowledge burst into flame in your heart."

Finder, Teacher, Matchmaker, Guide: Devotion to St. Anthony

♦ *By Norman Perry, O.F.M.*

*I*n the Basque region of Spain, St. Anthony of Padua is called *Santo Casamentero* or the Holy Matchmaker. In 1668, when he had already been dead four hundred years, the Spanish government by royal order made Anthony a soldier in its second infantry regiment. With each victory in which that regiment shared, Anthony was promoted in rank. He was finally retired after reaching general in 1889. In many European countries, Anthony is the patron of sailors and fishermen. Everywhere his intercession is invoked for the return of lost and stolen things.

He is also regarded as a patron of priests and travelers, a protector against the devil and guardian of the mails. He is called the wonder-worker and saint of the world.

The story and tradition of devotion to St. Anthony of Padua began almost with the moment of his death June 13, 1231. His Franciscan brothers tried to keep his death secret to avoid violence and a struggle between citizens of Padua and Capodi Porte to claim his body for burial. Despite their efforts to hide his death, children began running through the streets of Padua shouting, "The saint is dead!"

Crowds came to view the body of Anthony and attend his burial. His grave at once became a place of extraordinary devotion and numerous miracles. Legends would later attribute to him miracles worked even during his life.

Less than a month after his death the bishop, clergy, nobles and *podesta* or mayor of Padua requested his canonization. They gave among their reasons the great veneration and miracles taking place at his tomb. Anthony was not yet dead a year when Pope Gregory IX declared him a Saint of the Church and construction began on a basilica to honor his memory and remains. A papal bull dated two days before the first anniversary of his death granted an indulgence of one year to all who would visit Anthony's tomb on his feast or within its octave.

Since then popular piety and devotion to St. Anthony has taken many forms. In some cases history offers a reason for a particular practice or form of devotion. In other cases legends explain the devotions. And in some instances the origin of the devotion may be lost or unexplained.

Finder of Lost or Stolen Things

Nearly everywhere Anthony is asked to intercede with God for the return of things lost or stolen. Those who feel very familiar with him may pray, "Tony, Tony, turn around. Something's lost and must be found."

The reason for invoking St. Anthony's help in finding lost or stolen things is traced back to an incident in his own life. As the story goes, Anthony had a book of psalms that was very important to him. Besides the value of any book before the invention of printing, the psalter had the notes and comments he had made to use in teaching students in his Franciscan Order.

A novice who had already grown tired of living religious life decided to depart the community. Besides going AWOL he also took Anthony's psalter! Upon realizing his psalter was missing,

Anthony prayed it would be found or returned to him. And after his prayer the thieving novice was moved to return the psalter to Anthony and return to the Order which accepted him back. Legend has embroidered this story a bit. It has the novice stopped in his flight by a horrible devil brandishing an ax and threatening to trample him underfoot if he did not immediately return the book. Obviously a devil would hardly command anyone to do something good. But the core of the story would seem to be true. And the stolen book is said to be preserved in the Franciscan friary in Bologna.

In any event, shortly after his death people began praying through Anthony to find or recover lost and stolen articles. And the *Responsory of St. Anthony* composed by his contemporary, Julian of Spires, O.F.M., proclaims, "The sea obeys and fetters break/And lifeless limbs thou dost restore/While *treasures lost are found again*/When young or old thine aid implore."

The Novena to St. Anthony

In many churches and at shrines the world over, it is common to find not only a statue of St. Anthony but also the existence of a continuing novena in honor of the saint. People drop in and out of the devotions, making novenas on nine or thirteen Tuesdays or Sundays. An obvious reason for Tuesday is that Anthony was buried on a Tuesday and that is when the miracles began.

The novena in honor of St. Anthony, according to one or more novena books and leaflets, is linked with a legend about a pious childless couple in Bologna about the year 1617. The story says that after twenty-two years of longing for a child the wife took her troubles to St. Anthony. He is said to have appeared to her in a dream telling her, "For nine Tuesdays, one after the other, make visits to the church of my Order; on each of those days approach the holy sacraments of penance and of the altar, then pray before my picture, and what you ask, you shall obtain."

In one version of the story she conceived but gave birth to a badly deformed child. Again asking the saint's intercession, she touched the child, at Anthony's instruction, to his altar and the deformity at once disappeared.

Whatever fact may or may not be behind the legend, in 1898 Pope Leo XIII granted a plenary indulgence to those spending some time in devout meditation or prayers or performing some other acts

of piety in honor of St. Anthony of Padua on
Tuesday or Sunday of any week with the intention
of doing so for thirteen Tuesdays or Sundays
without interruption. At the same time Pope Leo
XIII recommended the practice of St. Anthony
Bread.

St. Anthony Bread

Different legends or stories account for the
donation of what is called St. Anthony Bread. By at
least one account it goes back to 1263, when it is
said a child drowned near the Basilica of St.
Anthony which was still being built. His mother
promised that if the child was restored to her she
would give for the poor an amount of corn equal to
the child's weight. Her prayer and promise were
rewarded with the boy's return to life.

Another reason for the practice is traced back to
a baker in France during 1890. Faced with a broken
lock on the shop door, the baker prayed through St.
Anthony that the locksmith could open the door
without breaking it down. She promised bread for
the poor in return for her favor. The door was
opened and she kept her promise.

Today the promise to give alms in honor of St.

Anthony if a favor is granted is called St. Anthony Bread. Sometimes the alms are given for the education of priests. In some places parents also make a gift for the poor after placing a newborn child under the protection of St. Anthony. It is a practice in some churches to bless small loaves of bread on the feast of St. Anthony and give them to those who want them.

St. Anthony Lilies

In many places lilies are blessed on the feast of St. Anthony and given to those who want them. Some people dry the lilies to preserve them or carry them on their person in a cloth container.

The lily is meant to remind the possessor of St. Anthony's purity and our own need to pray for the grace of purity in times of temptation.

This expression of piety is believed to have its roots in eighteenth-century France following the French Revolution. The Franciscans had been expelled from Corsica and their church abandoned. Yet people came to the church for an annual observance of the feast of St. Anthony on June 13. One year, some months after Anthony's feast, a man wandered into the church and found lilies from the celebration still fresh.

The custom of blessing lilies is another of those approved by Pope Leo XIII. The prayer of blessing asks for the grace to preserve chastity, peace and protection against the evil one.

St. Anthony's Brief

"Behold the Cross of the Lord! Begone, you enemy powers! The lion of the tribe of Juda, the root of David has conquered! Alleluia!" are words that Pope Sixtus V had inscribed on the obelisk he erected in the quadrangle in front of St. Peter's Basilica in Rome. They are also words attributed to St. Anthony known as the Brief (or letter) of St. Anthony. Some people carry the words with them asking for protection against the devil.

The custom of carrying and praying the words comes from the story of a woman in Portugal tempted by the devil and obsessed with thoughts of suicide. As the story is related, she was on her way to drown herself but stopped off at a Franciscan chapel to pray before a statue of St. Anthony. During her prayer she fell asleep and saw St. Anthony who released her from her disturbed state of mind. When she woke up she found a letter (brief) given to her by St. Anthony with the words quoted above. It has been written that the original letter was preserved with the crown jewels of Portugal. This practice may also be rooted in a story about Anthony's own struggle with the devil, who was trying to choke him. Anthony, says the early account by a contemporary friar, put the devil to flight by invoking Mary's help and making the Sign of the Cross.

Guardian of the Mails

Perhaps you've received a letter with the initials S.A.G. written somewhere on the envelope or under the flap or stamp. Or you may even have received a letter with a stamp bearing a picture of St. Anthony with the letters S.A.G. The letters stand for *St. Anthony Guide* or *Guard*. Usually the stamp has no more postal value than a Christmas or Easter seal. But in 1931, for the seventh centenary of Anthony's death, both Italy and Portugal issued postage stamps in his honor.

St. Anthony's association with the mail is said to have come from an incident in his life. According to a story in Charles Warren Stoddard's *St. Anthony: Wonder-Worker of Padua*, Anthony wished to journey to the town of Campo San Pietro, some distance from where he was staying. The purpose of the trip was to rest and reflect. He dutifully wrote a letter to his superior asking permission for the trip. But when it came time to give the letter to a messenger, the letter could not be found. Anthony took it as a sign he was not to go and put the trip from his mind. Inexplicably, some time later he received an answer from the superior giving permission for the trip.

A further association with the mail goes back to an event that was said to have happened in 1792. One Antonio Dante, so the story goes, journeyed to Lima, Peru, leaving his wife behind in Spain. After his departure she wrote to him many times without receiving any reply. Finally she went to the church of St. Francis in Oviedo and placed in the hands of St. Anthony's statue a letter to her husband in Peru. She prayed that Anthony would get the letter to him and obtain a reply.

The tale continues that she returned to the chapel the next day. A letter was still clasped in the hands of the statue. She began scolding St. Anthony for not delivering her letter. The noise she made brought the sacristan who said he had tried to get the letter from Anthony's hands without success.

The wife is then supposed to have reached up and quite easily taken the letter from Anthony's hands. At the same time three hundred gold coins spilled from the sleeve of the statue. When the letter was opened, it was not the wife's letter but a letter from the husband. He said that not hearing from her for so long he had thought her dead. But now her most recent letter had been delivered by a Franciscan priest.

Holy Matchmaker

As mentioned earlier, among the Basques, St. Anthony is called *Santo Casamentero*, the Holy Matchmaker or saint of those looking for husbands. According to a *Handbook of Christian Feasts and Customs* by Rev. Francis X. Weiser, published in 1958, Basque girls make a pilgrimage on Anthony's feast to his shrine in Durango. They pray that he will help them find "a good boy."

It may help that the young men are said to make the same journey to the shrine, where they wait outside the church until the young women are finished with their prayers to ask them to dance.

Weiser speculates that the association with engagement and marriage is inspired by all the statues and pictures of Anthony carrying the infant Jesus in his arms.

St. Anthony and the Child Jesus

St. Anthony has been pictured by artists and sculptors in all kinds of ways. He is depicted with a book in his hands, with a lily or torch. He has been painted preaching to fish, holding a monstrance with the Blessed Sacrament in front of a mule or preaching in the public square or from a nut tree.

But since the seventeenth century we most often find the saint shown with the child Jesus in his arms or even with the child standing on a book the saint holds. A story about St. Anthony related in the complete edition of *Butler's Lives of the Saints* (edited, revised and supplemented by Herbert Thurston, S.J., and Donald Attwater) projects back into the past a visit of Anthony to the Lord of Chatenauneuf. Anthony was praying far into the night when suddenly the room was filled with light more brilliant than the sun. Jesus then appeared to St. Anthony under the form of a little child. Chatenauneuf, attracted by the brilliant light that filled his house, was drawn to witness the vision but promised to tell no one of it until after

St. Anthony's death.

Some may see a similarity and connection between this story and the story in the life of St. Francis when he reenacted at Greccio the story of Jesus and the Christ Child became alive in his arms. There are other accounts of appearances of the child Jesus to Francis and some companions. These stories link Anthony with Francis in a sense of wonder and awe concerning the mystery of Christ's incarnation. They speak of a fascination with the humility and vulnerability of Christ who emptied himself to become one like us in all things except sin. For Anthony, like Francis, poverty was a way of imitating Jesus who was born in a stable and would have no place to lay his head.

The Chaplet of St. Anthony

Curious readers occasionally share descriptions or drawings of a chaplet of thirteen beads with a medal of St. Anthony. They want to know what kind of rosary or crown this may be. The beads are called the Chaplet of St. Anthony. The chaplet is prayed by saying an Our Father on the first bead, a Hail Mary on the second and a Glory Be on the third bead in each set. The chaplet seems to have had its origin in nineteenth-century Padua.

Patron of Sailors, Travelers and Fishermen

In Portugal, Italy, France and Spain, St. Anthony is
the patron saint of sailors and fishermen. According
to Father Weiser, his statue is sometimes placed in
a shrine on the ship's mast. And the sailors
sometimes scold him if he doesn't respond quickly
enough to their prayers.

Not only those who travel the seas but also other
travelers and vacationers pray that they may be kept
safe because of Anthony's intercession.

Several stories and legends may account for
associating the saint with travelers and sailors.

First, there is the very real fact of Anthony's
own travels in preaching the gospel, particularly his
journey and mission to preach the gospel in
Morocco, a mission cut short by severe illness. But
after his recovery and return to Europe he was a
man always on the go heralding the Good News.

There is also a story of two Franciscan sisters
who wished to make a pilgrimage to a shrine of our
Lady but did not know the way. A young man is
supposed to have volunteered to guide them. Upon
their return from the pilgrimage one of the sisters

announced that it was her patron saint, Anthony, who had guided them.

Still another story says that in 1647 Father Erastius Villani of Padua was returning by ship to Italy from Amsterdam. The ship with its crew and passengers was caught in a violent storm. All seemed doomed. Father Erastius encouraged everyone to pray to St. Anthony. Then he threw some pieces of cloth that had touched a relic of St. Anthony into the heaving seas. At once, the storm ended, the winds stopped and the sea became calm.

Teacher, Preacher, Doctor of the Scriptures

Among the Franciscans themselves and in the liturgy of his feast, St. Anthony is celebrated as a teacher and preacher extraordinaire. He was the first teacher in the Franciscan Order, given the special approval and blessing of St. Francis to instruct his brother Franciscans. His effectiveness as a preacher calling people back to the faith resulted in the title "Hammer of Heretics." Just as important were his peacemaking and calls for justice.

In canonizing Anthony in 1232, Pope Gregory IX spoke of him as the "Ark of the Testament" and

the "Respository of Holy Scripture." That explains
why St. Anthony is frequently pictured with a
burning light or a book of the Scriptures in his
hands. In 1946 Pope Pius XII officially declared
Anthony a Doctor of the Universal Church. It is in
Anthony's love of the word of God and his
prayerful efforts to understand and apply it to the
situations of everyday life that the Church
especially wants us to imitate St. Anthony. While
noting in the prayer of his feast Anthony's
effectiveness as an intercessor, the Church
especially wants us to learn from Anthony, the
teacher, the meaning of true wisdom and what it
means to become like Jesus who humbled and
emptied himself for our sakes and went about doing
good.

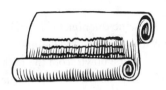

The Great Virtues of St. Anthony

♦ *By Leonard Foley, O.F.M.*

S aints, of course, are virtuous across the board. But there is a wonderful kaleidoscope of particular emphases in the life of each. In St. Anthony's case popular piety has singled out the following:

Contemplation

St. Anthony longed for solitude, like St. Francis. After he had worked hard in preaching the Gospel, he would always feel the need for quiet, undisturbed prayer. He spoke from experience:

"When one withdraws from the turbulence of the world and rests in quiet and solitude, tasting the bread of tears as he thinks over his sins and relishing the delights of heaven—then does the Lord make himself known to him."

He felt the same dilemma as Francis: Should he give himself to prayer or to teaching? Like Jesus, who, he said, "came down from the Father for the salvation of souls," he was willing to sacrifice the quiet of prayer and take upon himself the toilsome apostolate of preaching. But as often as he could, he would climb a mountain to where the Benedictines had given the friars a small chapel, with caves in the side of the mountain. Here he could look down on the beauties of Umbria and praise God as the mighty creator of this wondrous world.

Zeal

St. Anthony chose Padua as his place of residence when he was thirty-four—two years before his death, and in that short time became the inspiration of the whole city. His very first sermon won for him the affection of the crowds, and he would go into the great piazzas of the city or to the fields outside.

Courage

St. Anthony fearlessly faced the heretics of his day, preaching in the hotbeds of the Albigensians. In Padua, there were constant wars with the tyrant

Ezzelino of Verona, a ruthless and brutal man. When a certain count, the head of the Guelph (papal) party, was captured by Ezzelino, St. Anthony went straight into the tyrant's camp to get the prisoner released. This time, however, in spite of St. Anthony's strong language, Ezzelino would not budge. Saints do not always succeed, and St. Anthony was so depressed by the failure of this mission that after his return to Padua he retired into solitude and devoted himself to contemplation.

Peacemaker

St. Francis said to his friars, "Go, my beloved brothers, two by two to the four corners of the world and announce the message of peace and penance for the forgiveness of sins." As a result of Anthony's preaching, quarrels were patched up, mortal enemies reconciled, poor debtors were released from prison and given their freedom, and restitution was made for stolen goods. His main concern, of course, was to bring people back to peace with God. After a sermon he would go into the confessional, sometimes having to remain there for the rest of the day.

Friend of the Poor

In St. Anthony's day, a debtor who could not pay might be imprisoned for his debt, this in keeping with pagan-Roman law. St. Anthony's influence paved the way for a new law whereby a debtor did not lose his personal freedom.

He condemned excessive interest charges and used an earthy example for the folly of greed. "A miser is like a tumblebug which gathers dung and with much labor makes it into a ball. Then an ass comes along, steps on the beetle and its ball, and annihilates both. This is what happens to the miser and the usurer."

Mary

As Anthony was dying he sang the well-known hymn of his day, *O Gloriosa Virginis*:

> O Glorious Lady, exalted high in heaven
>   above,
> The great Creator, mighty Lord,
> Was nursed by thee with mother's love.
> What sinful Eve had lost of us,
> by thy dear Son thou didst restore.

Part Two:
Praying to St. Anthony

Praying to the Saints

*T*oday, devotions to St. Anthony seem to have declined, although novena prayers are still faithfully said in many churches after the Tuesday morning Mass and during the nine-week novena before his feast, June 13.

The explanation for this is no doubt complex: One reason may be the rise of new emphases in spirituality—the charismatic movement, Marriage Encounter, prayer groups and Bible study groups, the seeking for more spontaneous and creative forms of prayer; another may be greater education and, for some, a rise in the standard of living that possibly has led to a greater sense of independence.

Most importantly, however, Catholics were reminded with great emphasis that the central act of their faith, and the source of all spirituality, is the Mass. Jesus is the Lord of all, and the Church gathers around him. The Eucharist is not one of many equal devotions in the Church; it is the supreme act of our faith.

Churches built with this realization now have an almost obsessive concern that everything in the Church must focus on the altar. To the disappointment of many, this makes for a severe simplicity, almost a coldness. Statues of the saints are seen by some liturgists as a distraction.

(Vatican II did say, "The placing of sacred images in churches so that they may be venerated by the faithful is to be maintained. Nevertheless their number should be moderate and their relative positions should reflect right order. For otherwise the Christian people may find them incongruous and they may foster devotion of a doubtful orthodoxy" [*Constitution on the Liturgy*, 125].)

It's not that there has been a set determination to downgrade the saints. Rather, it was the emphasis on the centrality of Jesus. This unavoidably caused a lessening of attention paid to the saints, including even Mary.

It is human and understandable that we blame Vatican II for whatever we don't like about the Church today. But there is nothing in the Council documents that downgrades devotion to the saints, except an admonition: "Let the faithful remember moreover that true devotion consists neither in sterile or transitory affection, nor in a certain vain credulity, but proceeds from true faith" (*Constitution on the Church*, 67).

In the document just quoted, the pope and bishops said that when we look at the lives of those who have faithfully followed Christ, we are inspired to seek "the city which is to come." In the lives of those who shared in our humanity and yet were transformed into specially successful images of Christ, God vividly manifests his presence and his face. Moreover, when we cherish the memory of the saints, the union of the whole Church is strengthened. Our communion with each other on earth brings us closer to Christ.

"It is supremely fitting, therefore, that we love those friends and fellow heirs of Jesus Christ, who are also our brothers and sisters and extraordinary benefactors, and that we give thanks to God for them" (excerpted from *Constitution on the Church*, 50).

Traditional Novena to St. Anthony

S t. Anthony is a favorite saint of the people. He is called the Wonder Worker because of the many miracles with which God has favored him. He has traditionally been the refuge of all who have lost things, whether temporal or spiritual.

An excellent expression of devotion to St. Anthony is the making of a novena, nine or thirteen Tuesdays or nine consecutive days of prayer, public or private, for a certain intention. A novena differs from an octave in that it precedes, rather than follows, a saint's feast. Tuesday is especially honored in devotion to St. Anthony because his burial day, June 17, 1231, fell on a Tuesday.

Novenas began in Spain and France in preparation for the feast of Christmas, the number representing the nine months Jesus lived in the womb of his mother. The practice spread to the feasts of Mary and the saints.

Novenas have been attacked as superstitious, partly because of the special efficacy that some people attach to the number nine. This, of course, must be guarded against. No greater efficacy should be attributed to novena prayers as such than to any devout prayer earnestly and perseveringly undertaken.

Perseverance and constancy are qualities of all good prayer; hence it is good to give special emphasis to them by requiring repetition on certain days. This shows the worshiper's earnestness and fervor.

To make a novena to St. Anthony, use any of the prayers in this booklet.

How to Join the Novena of the National Shrine of St. Anthony

On any Tuesday you may join those making a novena at the National Shrine of St. Anthony in Cincinnati, Ohio, by reciting and continuing to pray the prayers here for nine consecutive Tuesdays. Mass is offered for benefactors in the Shrine chapel every Tuesday, or you may wish to attend Mass in your own church on that day. In God's own way, we are always blessed by this perseverance and trust.

If you wish, send your petition to be placed at the Shrine by writing it on a piece of paper and placing it in a sealed envelope marked *My Petition to St. Anthony*. You may also put your initials and city (e.g., J.B., Tampa) on the envelope. Mail it in another envelope to St. Anthony Messenger, Shrine Department, 1615 Republic St., Cincinnati, OH 45210.

Each month a list of favors granted is published in *St. Anthony Messenger* for those who wish to publicly acknowledge they have been blessed through the prayers of St. Anthony.

The Responsory of St. Anthony

If you ask for miracles,
Death, error, all calamities,
The leprosy and demons fly,
And health succeeds infirmities.

The sea obeys, and fetters break,
And lifeless limbs thou dost restore;
Whilst treasures lost are found again
When young or old thine aid implore.

All dangers vanish at thy prayer,
And direst need doth quickly flee.
Let those who know thy power
    proclaim—
Let Paduans say—These are of thee.

The sea obeys...

To Father, Son, may glory be,
And Holy Ghost eternally.

The sea obeys...

Verse: Pray for us, blessed Anthony:
Response: That we may be made worthy
of the promises of Christ.

Let your Church, O God, be made joyful
by the solemn commemoration of
blessed Anthony, your confessor and
doctor; that the Church may always be
defended by your spiritual help, and
merit to possess eternal joys. Through
Christ our Lord. Amen.

Prayer to Find What Is Lost

Since your death, St. Anthony, the Lord
has worked countless wonders and
answered countless people's prayers
because of your loving prayer for them.
Those who have experienced the power
of prayer offered through you have told
how God was pleased to help them in
their need, restoring peace of mind,
healing the sick, finding what was lost,
spiritual or material. Now in our need
we ask you to pray for each of us that we
may continue to share in God's loving
care and protection and through you be
drawn to eternal life. Amen.

or

St. Anthony, when you prayed
   your stolen book of prayers was given
   back to you.
Pray now for all of us who have lost
   things precious and dear.
Pray for all who have lost faith, hope or
   the friendship of God.
Pray for us who have lost friends or
   relatives by death.
Pray for all who have lost peace of mind
   or spirit.
Pray that we may be given new hope,
   new faith, new love.
Pray that lost things, needful and
   helpful to us, may be returned to our
   keeping.
Or, if we must continue in our loss,
   pray that we may be given Christ's
   comfort and peace. Amen.

Prayer for Poor Children

St. Anthony, your love for the infant
Jesus, made him present to you to see
and hold in your arms. Help us to see
and love Jesus in all the poor and
suffering of the world. Move us to
clothe, feed and help Jesus, in all
unwanted, abused and abandoned
children and people. Lead us, for the
sake of Jesus who became a child like
one of us, to reverence and protect all
human life from its beginning to its end.
Amen.

Prayer of Thanksgiving

St. Anthony, God has helped me
abundantly through your prayer and has
strengthened me in my need. I thank
God and I thank you. Accept this prayer
and my serious resolve which I now
renew to live always in the love of Jesus
and of my neighbor. Continue to shield
me by your protection and pray to God
for the final grace of one day entering
the kingdom of heaven to sing with you
the everlasting mercies of God. Amen.

Prayer to St. Anthony, 'The Wonder Worker'

After you died, St. Anthony, God chose to make your holiness known to the world and to draw people by working miracles in answer to prayers made through your intercession. Since then people have asked God to continue to honor you by working wonders through your intercession. Those who have experienced the power of prayers offered through your intercession have told how God has answered them. God has healed the sick, restored peace of mind, relieved poverty and granted favors of all kinds. Now in my (our) time of need, I (we) ask you, St. Anthony, to pray with me (us) for the things I (we) desire. I (we) pray that God may again give us a sign of loving care and providence and that, through you, God may draw us all to eternity. Amen.

More Prayers to St. Anthony

St. Anthony is variously portrayed in sculpture and painting with several symbols. These often help us to pray in his spirit.

St. Anthony Holding the Child Jesus

Blessed Anthony, Jesus was the center of your life. It must be the same for me, for every Christian. Your purity of soul, your humbleness, your simple radiant faith fits well with the gentle and humble Savior, who was a little child to his Father in heaven. Help us to give up our desire for power and control. Keep us from a merely intellectual faith and may we be totally dependent on Jesus as you were, with the helplessness of a little child. Amen.

St. Anthony With the Book

Blessed Anthony, the Lord made the
Scriptures a glowing flame in your mind
and heart. Your sermons were filled
with the words of the Lord. May we
listen to the same Lord speaking to us in
the Bible with the same reverent
openness as you had. May we feel the
presence of Jesus in the Scriptures just
like the people of your day, when you
preached that word to them. Amen.

St. Anthony With the Flaming Torch and Burning Heart

St. Anthony, we marvel at your enthusiasm, especially in your years of preaching. Your hours of prayer set you on fire to use your great talent in tireless preaching, even though it damaged your health in your last days. May our devotion to you awaken our cold hearts, sated with the creature comforts and distractions of our day. May the presence of Jesus in our prayer warm us to genuine love for others. Give us the courage and ardor to stand for the truth, whatever the cost. Amen.

St. Anthony Holding a Lily

St. Anthony, you were truly spoken of
by Jesus, when he said, "Blessed are the
pure of heart, the singleminded." Your
faith and love of Jesus made you respect
and honor God's beautiful creation, our
bodies, made in the image of Jesus.
Your mind and heart were free of all
double-dealing with God and with your
brothers and sisters. His love shone
through you as through crystals. Help us
also to be pure of heart and mind, with
whole-hearted love of God. Amen.

St. Anthony Holding the Cross

St. Anthony, you raised the cross before sinners and saints, to be a sign of the price God paid to show us his love, to be our only hope of salvation and to give us courage in suffering. You always preached penance—a turning away from anyone and anything that separates us from God, even slightly. You put the First Thing first—the dying of Jesus, given to us that we might enter into his spirit as he died—and his resurrection, which he wills to share with us. Help us to die to sin, large and small, and by this dying to be lifted up in grace—once for all as we die and many times throughout our days. Amen.

St. Anthony, Instrument of Justice and Peace

St. Anthony, during your life you
imitated St. Francis of Assisi in his love
for Gospel poverty and for the poor.
While you desired little for yourself,
you were constantly alive to the needs
of the poor and little people of the
world. You shared what you had with
them and demanded justice for them.
We ask now, in your name, that we may
not be overly desirous of wealth or
possessions. May we share what we
have with others less fortunate. Make us
always instruments and voices for peace
and justice in our world. Amen.

St. Anthony Bread

"**S**t. Anthony Bread" is a term used for offerings made in thanksgiving to God for blessings received through the prayers of St. Anthony.

The term and practice seems to have begun by Louise Bouffier, a shopkeeper in Toulon, France. A locksmith was prepared to break open her shop door after no key would open it. Bouffier asked the locksmith to try his keys one more time after she prayed and promised to give bread to the poor in honor of St. Anthony if the door would open without force. The door then opened. After others received favors through the intercession of St. Anthony, they joined Louise Bouffier in founding the charity of St. Anthony Bread.

For over one hundred years, St. Anthony Messenger has been a popular place to send St. Anthony Bread. You may wish to send your offering, designated as St. Anthony Bread, to

St. Anthony Bread, *St. Anthony Messenger*, 1615 Republic St., Cincinnati, OH 45210. Your alms will be used to help men preparing to be Franciscan brothers and priests and to help the poor, especially those to whom the Franciscans minister.

The National Shrine of St. Anthony

♦ *Franciscan Friars, 5000 Colerain Ave.,*
Cincinnati, OH 45223 (513) 541-2146

History of the National Shrine

A devout member of St. Francis Seraph parish in
Cincinnati, Ohio, A. Joseph Nurre, and his wife
bought a country estate high above the city for the
Franciscan friars. The Nurres promised to build a
monastery, a home for infirm friars and a chapel to
serve as a Franciscan novitiate. The cornerstone
was laid in 1888 and blessed by Fr. Jerome
Kilgenstein, O.F.M., the first provincial superior of
the Cincinnati friars. In October, the first friars
moved into the original estate house, and on
Thanksgiving Day 1889, Archbishop Henry Elder
of Cincinnati consecrated the chapel. The first
investitures at Mt. Airy, the familiar name for the
friary and shrine, took place on the feast of the

Assumption in 1890.

The chapel, although dedicated to St. Anthony, was never intended to become a shrine. Gradually, however, people began to make private pilgrimages to the chapel and as the number of visitors increased, the chapel became known as St. Anthony's Shrine. Furnishings for the Shrine came from France, Belgium, Bavaria, Holland and Austria. Originally the shrine contained eight side altars. Above the high altar were two large paintings portraying scenes from the life of St. Anthony; these paintings, however, were covered over when the shrine was redecorated in 1978.

In January 1928, a small group of friends met at the friary at the invitation of Fr. Stephen Hoffmann, O.F.M., to establish a society to further the devotion to St. Anthony and to maintain the shrine. The society built a beautiful shelterhouse for serving refreshments to visitors, which has since been replaced by the present hall. The society also welcomes and accommodates visitors and organizes the annual festival in September.